W9-DCO-756

Tasting

Inquiries should be addressed to Raintree Childrens Books, 205 West Highland Avenue, Milwaukee, Wisconsin 53203.

Library of Congress Number: 79-29662

2 3 4 5 6 7 8 9 0 84 83 82

Printed in the United States of America.

Library of Congress Cataloging in Publication Data

Allington, Richard L
Tasting.

(Beginning to learn about)
SUMMARY: Introduces the 4 basic tastes, sweet, sour, bitter, and salty, along with 15 other types of tastes and textures, such as spicy, cold, and crunchy. Recipes and activities are included.
1. Taste — Juvenile literature. [1. Taste]
I. Cowles, Kathleen, joint author. II. Spangler, Noel. III. Title. IV. Series.
QP456.A44 152.1'67 79-29662
ISBN 0-8172-1292-2 lib. bdg.

Richard L. Allington is Associate Professor, Department of Reading, State University of New York at Albany.
Kathleen Cowles is the author of several picture books.

BEGINNING TO LEARN ABOUT

TASTING

BY RICHARD L. ALLINGTON, PH.D., • AND KATHLEEN COWLES

ILLUSTRATED BY NOEL SPANGLER

Raintree Childrens Books • Milwaukee • Toronto • Melbourne • London

I used to eat baby food —
mashed-up this . . .
squishy that . . .
warm milk.
After a while, it all tastes the same.

Now I eat all kinds of food.
Everything tastes different.

I taste with my tongue.

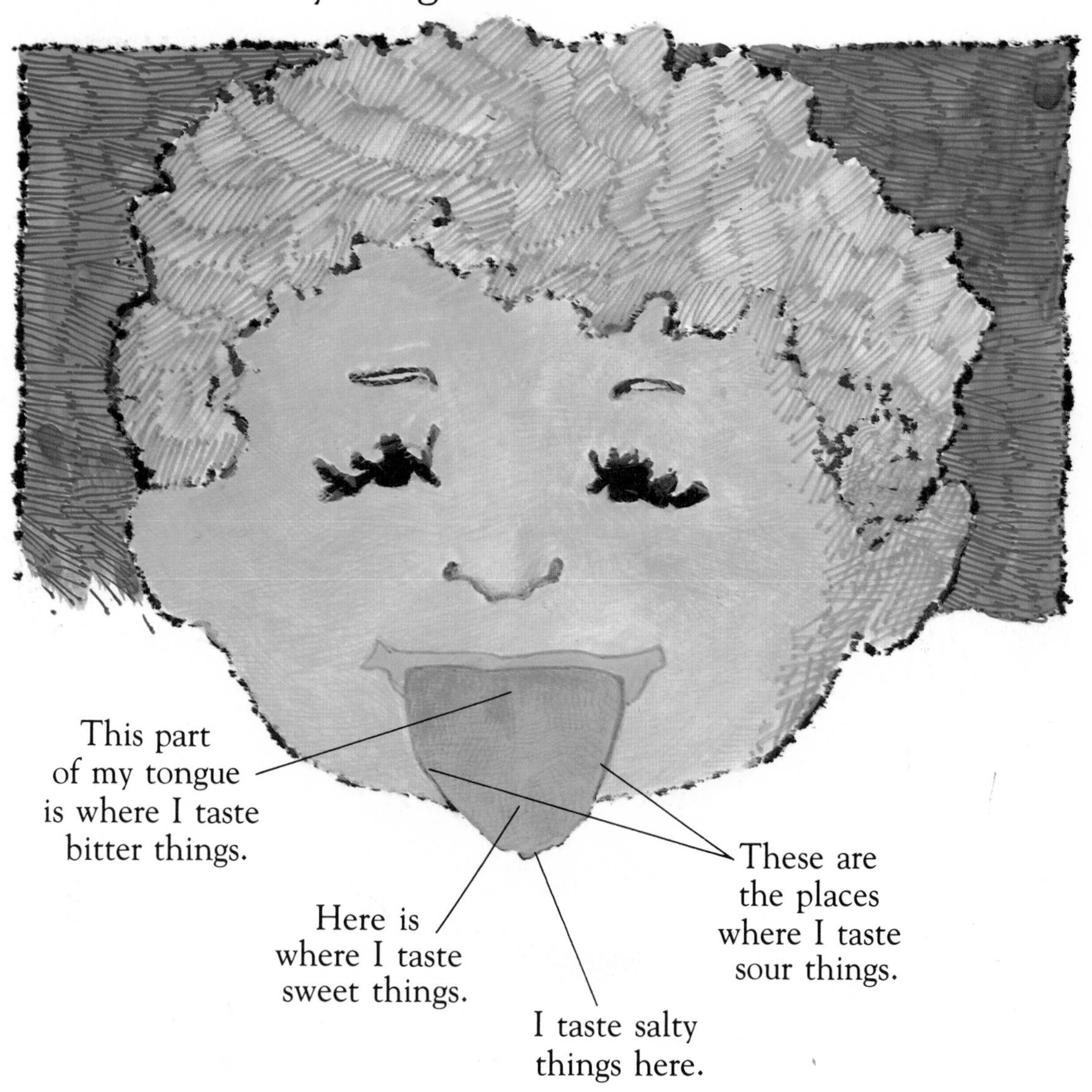

I taste sweet things and sour things.
Which things taste sweet to you?
Which things taste sour?

dill
pickle
vinegar
honey
mint
raisins
peach
watermelon

I taste bitter things and salty things.
Which things taste bitter to you?
Which things taste salty?

tea
unsweetened chocolate
cheese
salt
chicken

I TASTE A SALAD.

You may ask an adult to help you with this recipe for Sweet Fruit Salad.

1. For each person, peel 1 banana. Cut it into bite-size pieces. Put them into a small bowl.

2. Then choose 1 of the following:

10 raisins

OR
5 green grapes
(rinse them off with water)

OR 1 spoonful of your favorite berries, fresh or frozen (if fresh, rinse them off with water)

3. Add your choice to the banana in the bowl. Add 1 spoonful of honey. Mix well.

I TASTE A SALAD DRESSING.

You may ask an adult to help you with this recipe for Sweet and Sour Salad Dressing.

1. For each serving, put 1 spoonful of lemon juice into a small bowl.

2. Then put in 2 spoonfuls of water.

3. Add a spoonful of honey.

4. Then add 1 shake of salt and 1 shake of pepper.

5. Stir it well.

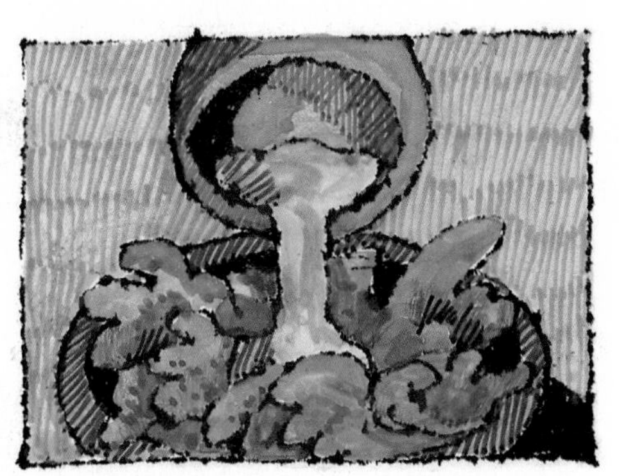

6. Pour it on the Sweet Fruit Salad, or on your favorite kind of green salad.

I taste spicy things and bland things.
Which things taste spicy to you?
Which things taste bland?

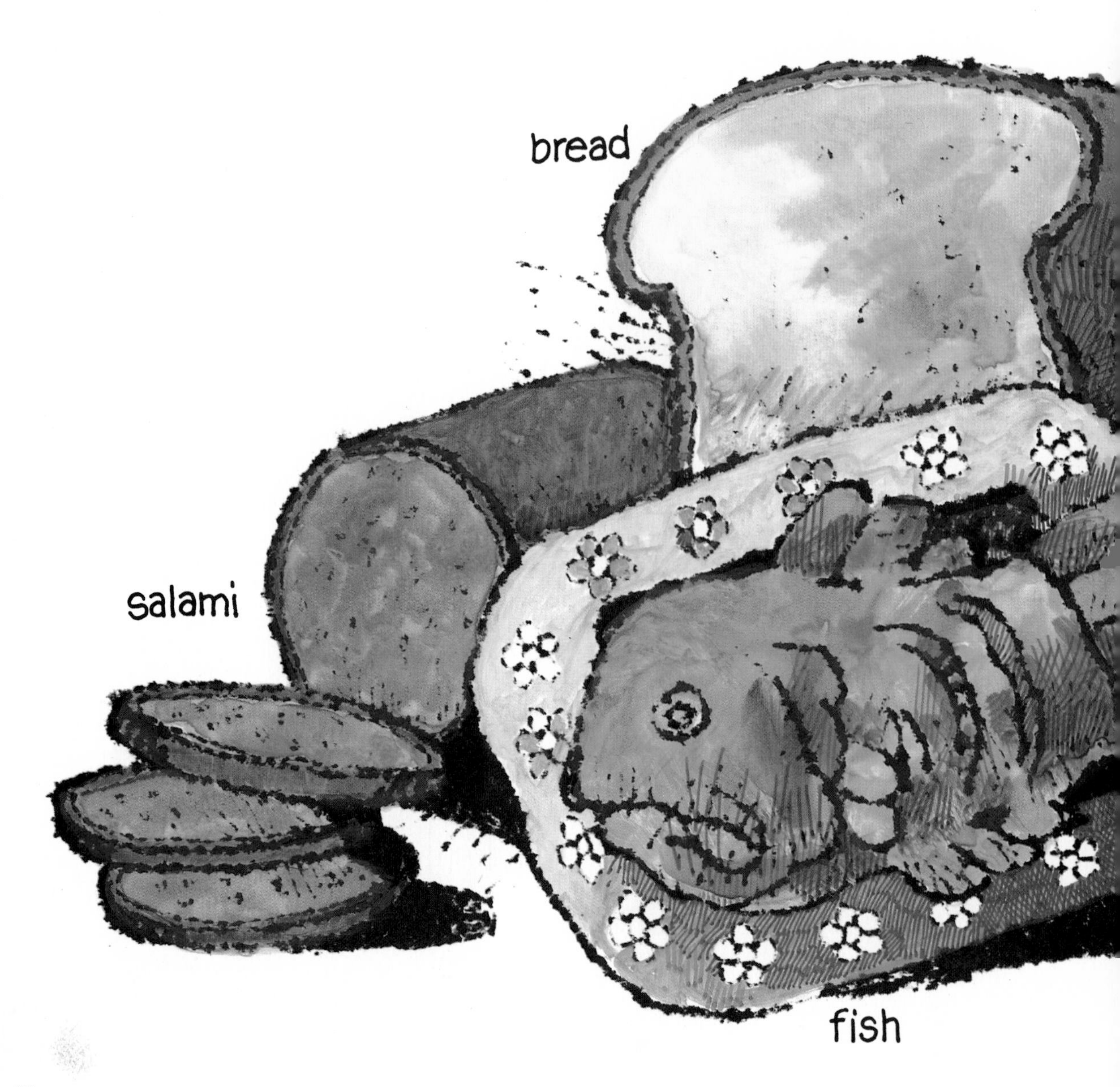

catsup
banana
rice
onion
potato

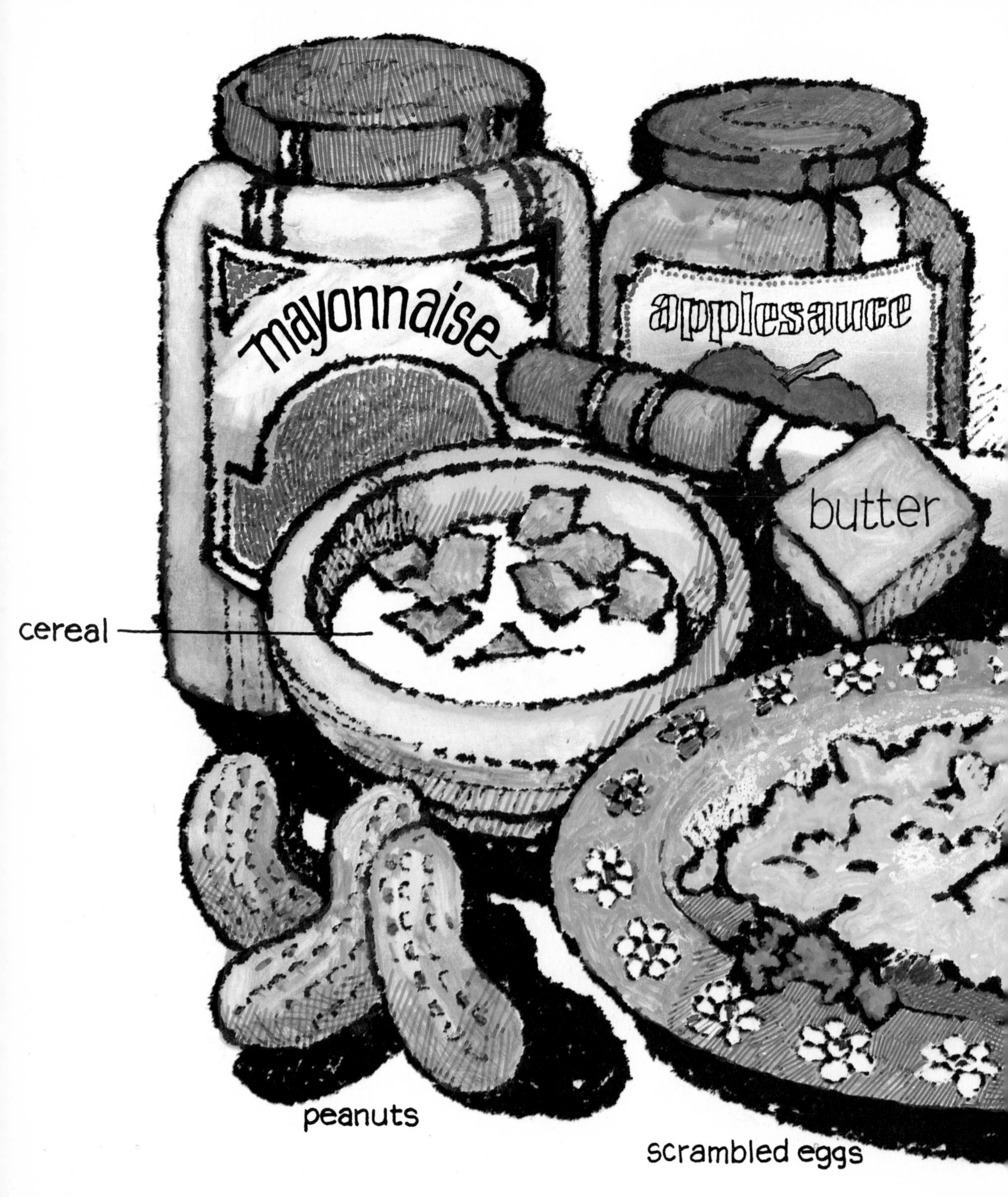
mayonnaise
applesauce
butter
cereal
peanuts
scrambled eggs

My tongue tells me how food feels.
Which things feel lumpy to you?
Which things feel smooth?
Which things feel crunchy?

I TASTE SNACKS.

You may ask an adult to help you with this recipe for Spicy Snacks.

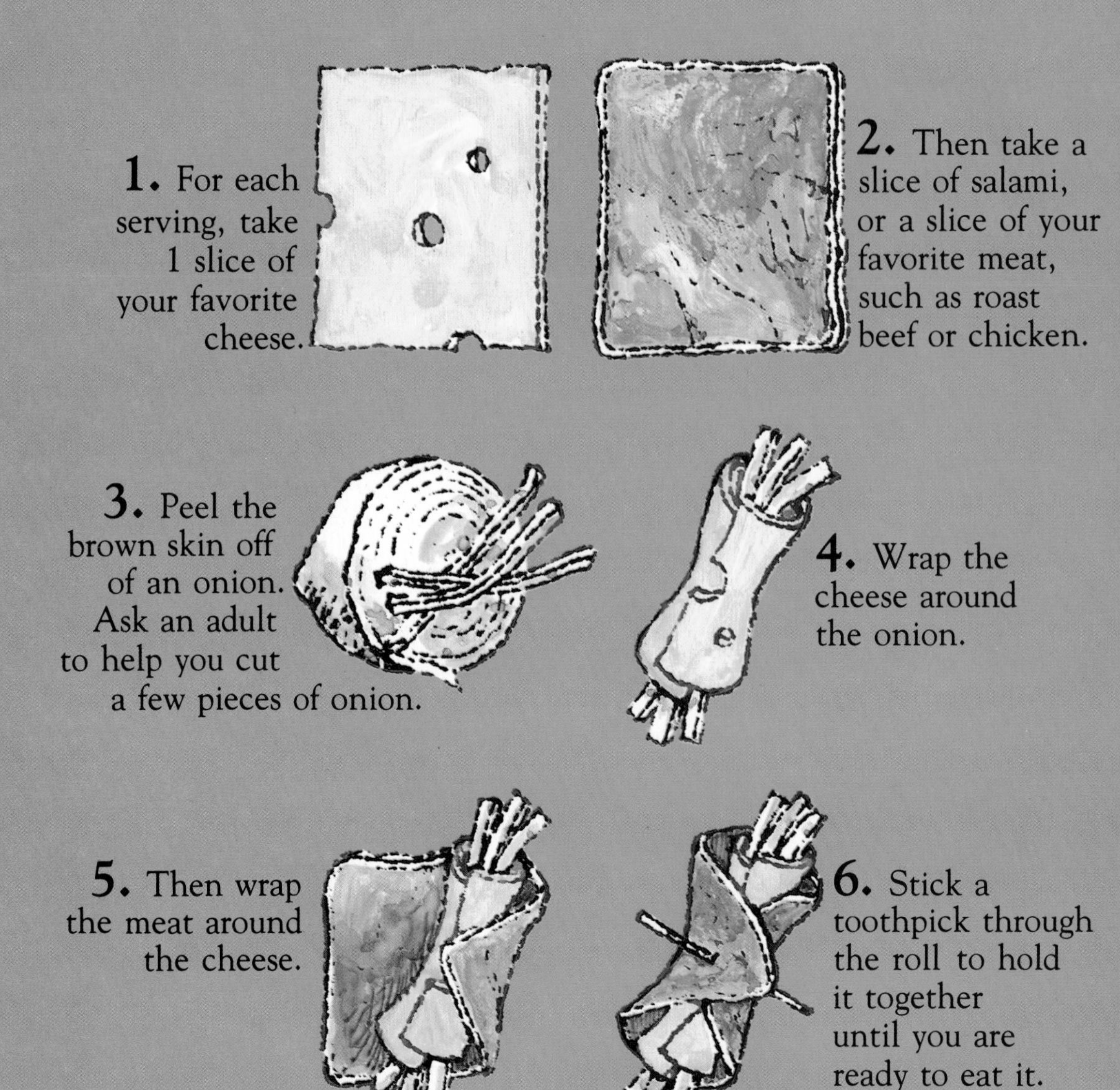

1. For each serving, take 1 slice of your favorite cheese.
2. Then take a slice of salami, or a slice of your favorite meat, such as roast beef or chicken.
3. Peel the brown skin off of an onion. Ask an adult to help you cut a few pieces of onion.
4. Wrap the cheese around the onion.
5. Then wrap the meat around the cheese.
6. Stick a toothpick through the roll to hold it together until you are ready to eat it.

You may ask an adult to help you with this recipe for Crunchy Snacks. As with all the recipes in this book, be sure to wash your hands before starting.

1. For each serving, put 3 spoonfuls of crunchy peanut butter into a bowl.

2. Mix the peanut butter with 1 spoonful of honey.

3. With your fingers, roll this mix into a ball. Set it aside.

4. Into the bowl, pour 2 spoonfuls of your favorite cereal or your favorite kind of seeds.

5. Roll the peanut butter ball around the bowl until it is completely covered with cereal or seeds.

Which things feel hot when you eat them?

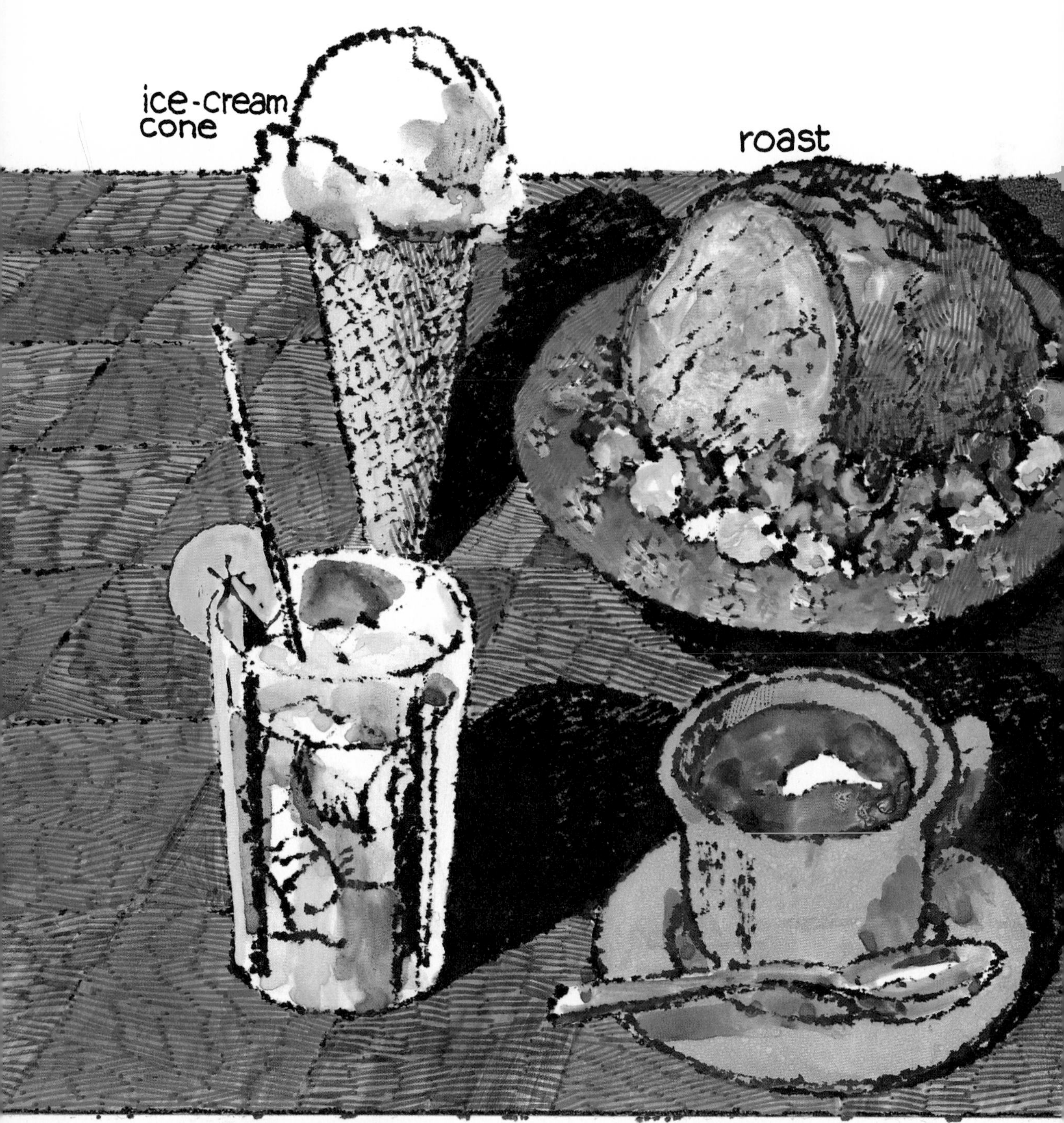

Which things feel cold?

Which things feel crisp to you?
Which things feel soggy?

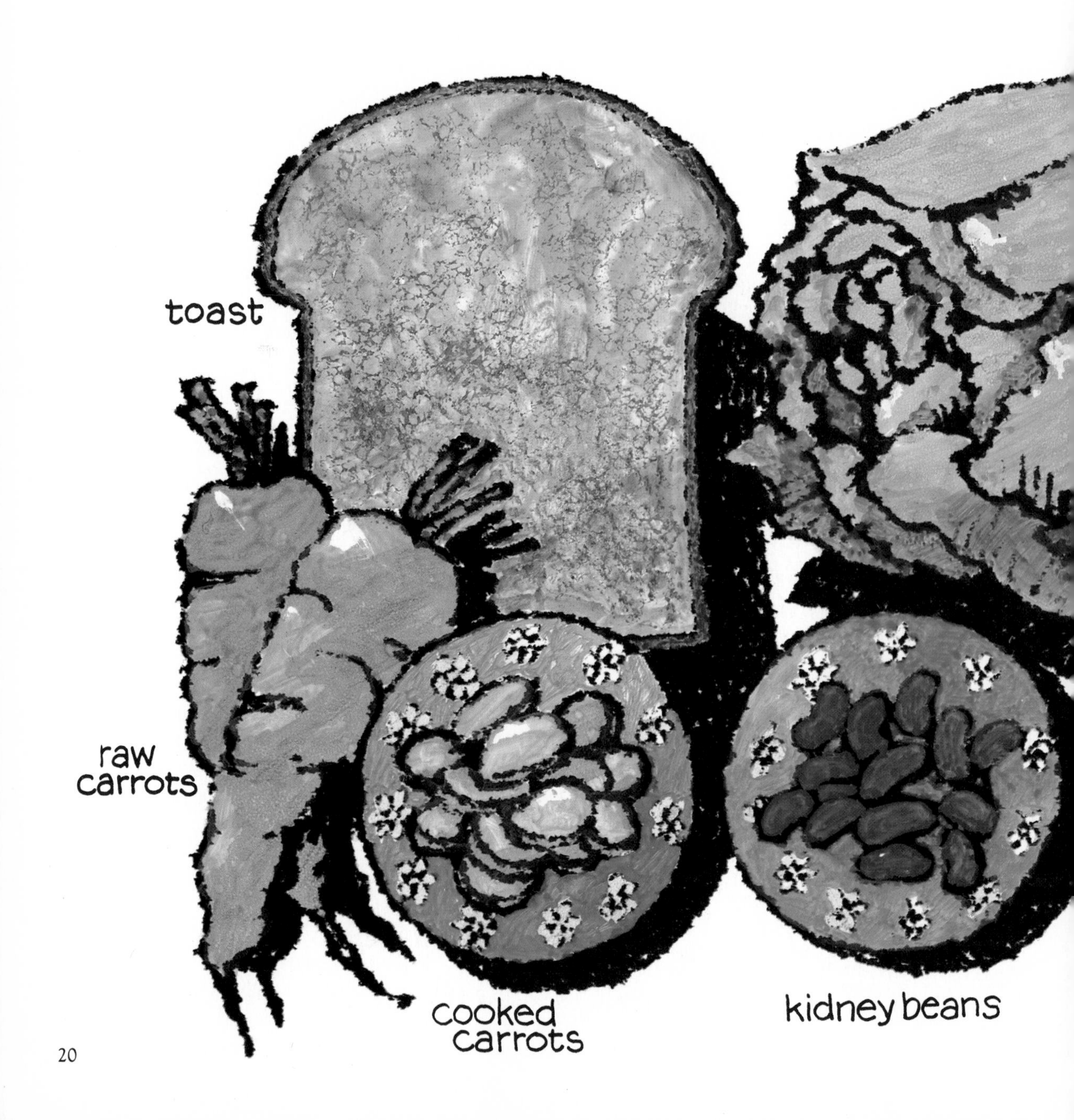

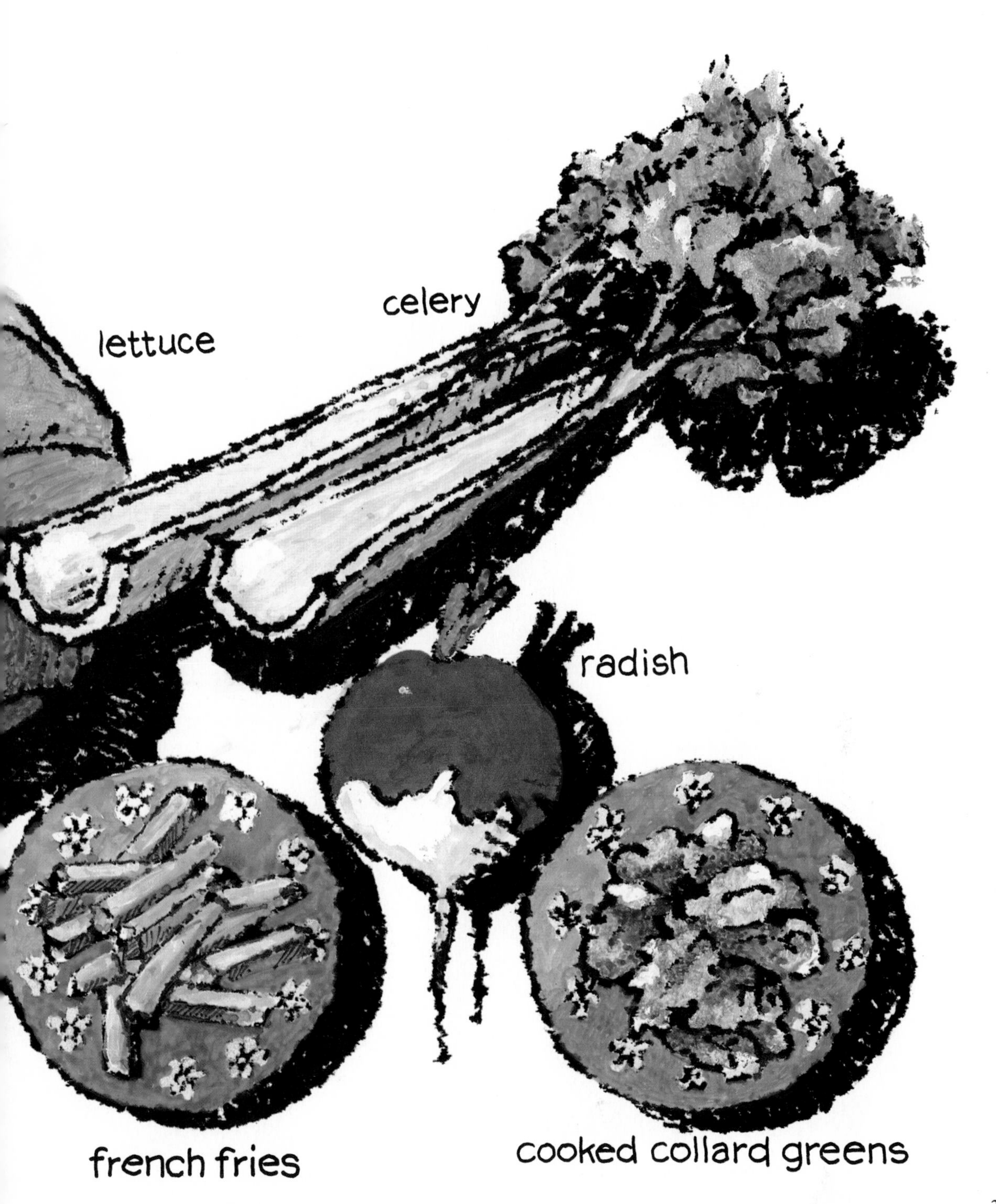
celery
lettuce
radish
french fries
cooked collard greens

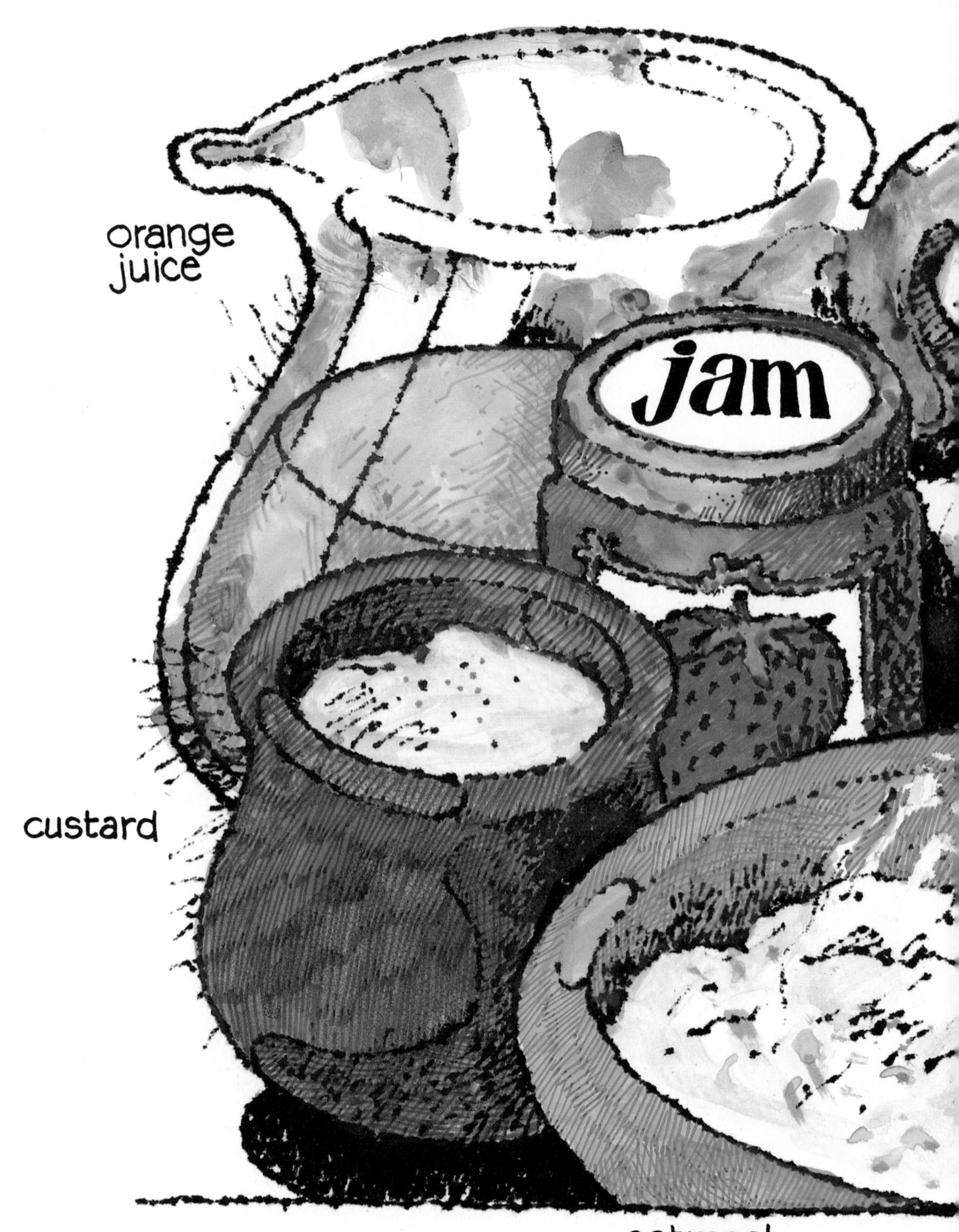
orange juice
jam
custard
oatmeal

Which things feel thick to you?
Which things feel thin?

I TASTE A SANDWICH.

You may ask an adult to help you with this recipe for Crispy Sandwich.

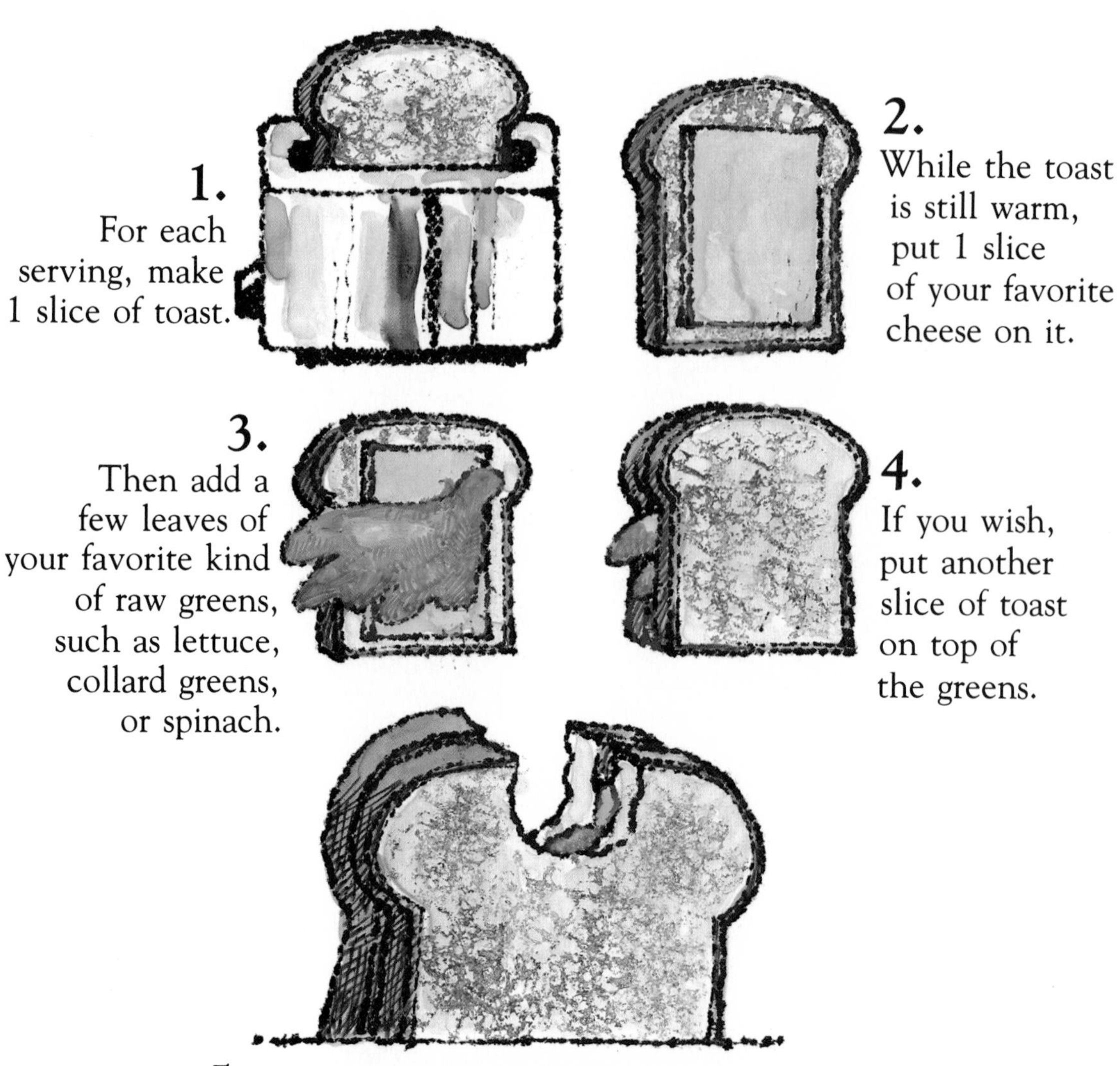

1. For each serving, make 1 slice of toast.

2. While the toast is still warm, put 1 slice of your favorite cheese on it.

3. Then add a few leaves of your favorite kind of raw greens, such as lettuce, collard greens, or spinach.

4. If you wish, put another slice of toast on top of the greens.

5. Eat the sandwich while it is still warm.

I TASTE A SNACK.
You may ask an adult to help you
with this recipe for Sweet and Salty Snacks.

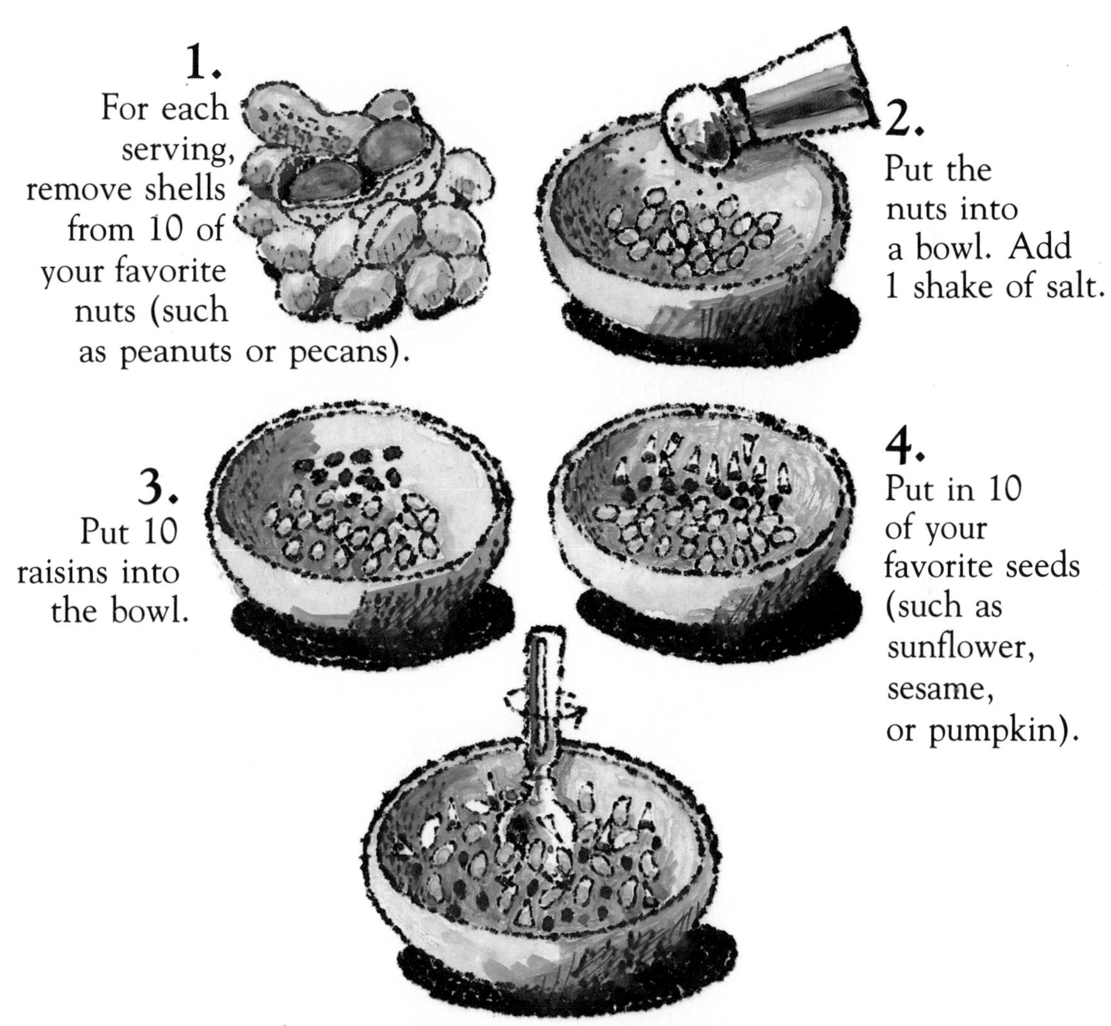

1. For each serving, remove shells from 10 of your favorite nuts (such as peanuts or pecans).

2. Put the nuts into a bowl. Add 1 shake of salt.

3. Put 10 raisins into the bowl.

4. Put in 10 of your favorite seeds (such as sunflower, sesame, or pumpkin).

5. Stir the mixture well with a spoon.

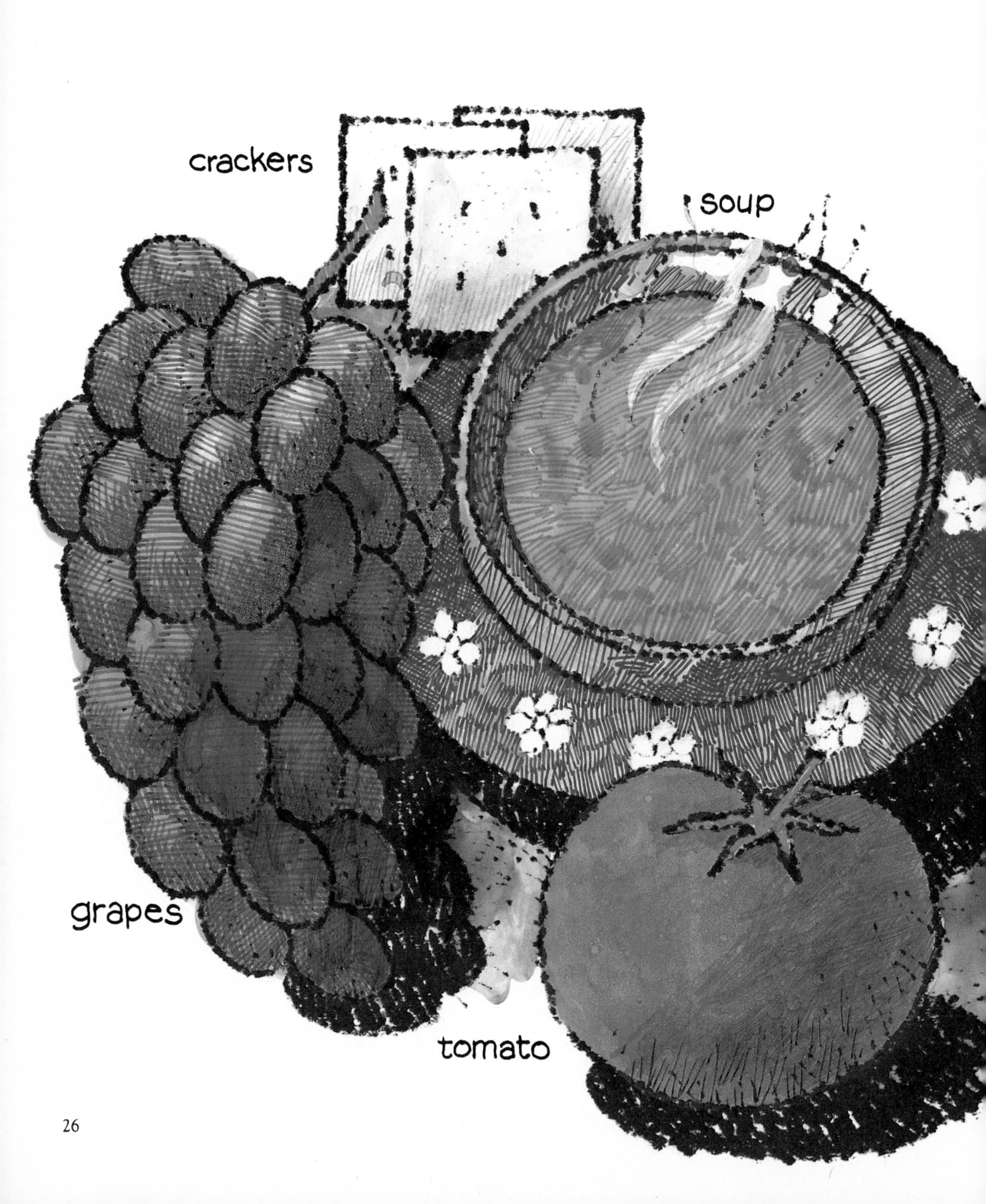
crackers
soup
grapes
tomato

Which things feel dry when you eat them?
Which things feel wet?

Which things are liquid?

Which things are solid?

I TASTE A SANDWICH.
You may ask an adult to help you with this recipe for a Wet and Dry Sandwich.

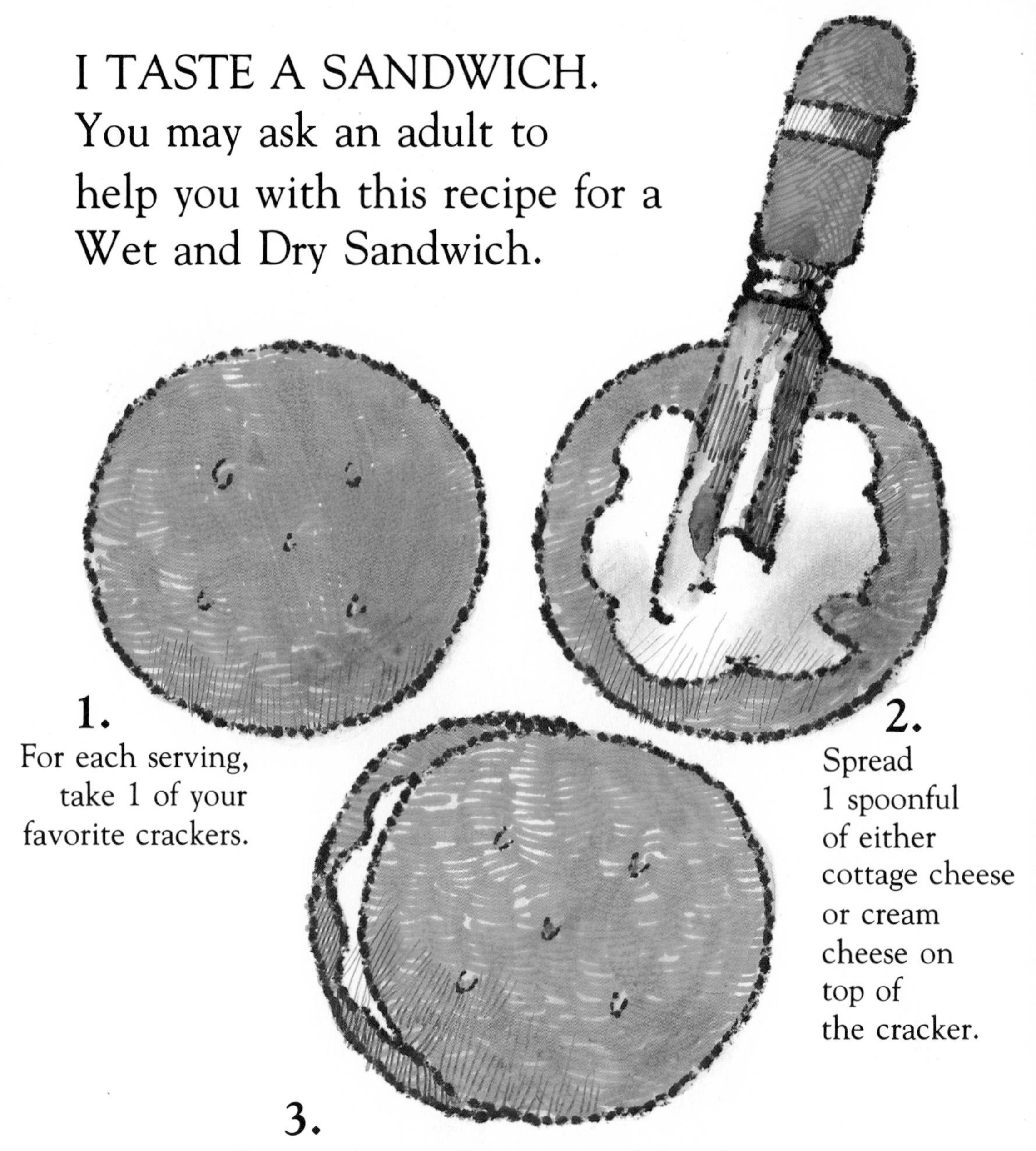

1.
For each serving, take 1 of your favorite crackers.

2.
Spread 1 spoonful of either cottage cheese or cream cheese on top of the cracker.

3.
Put another cracker on top of the cheese.

I TASTE A DESSERT.

You may ask an adult to help you with this recipe for Fruit Ice Cubes.

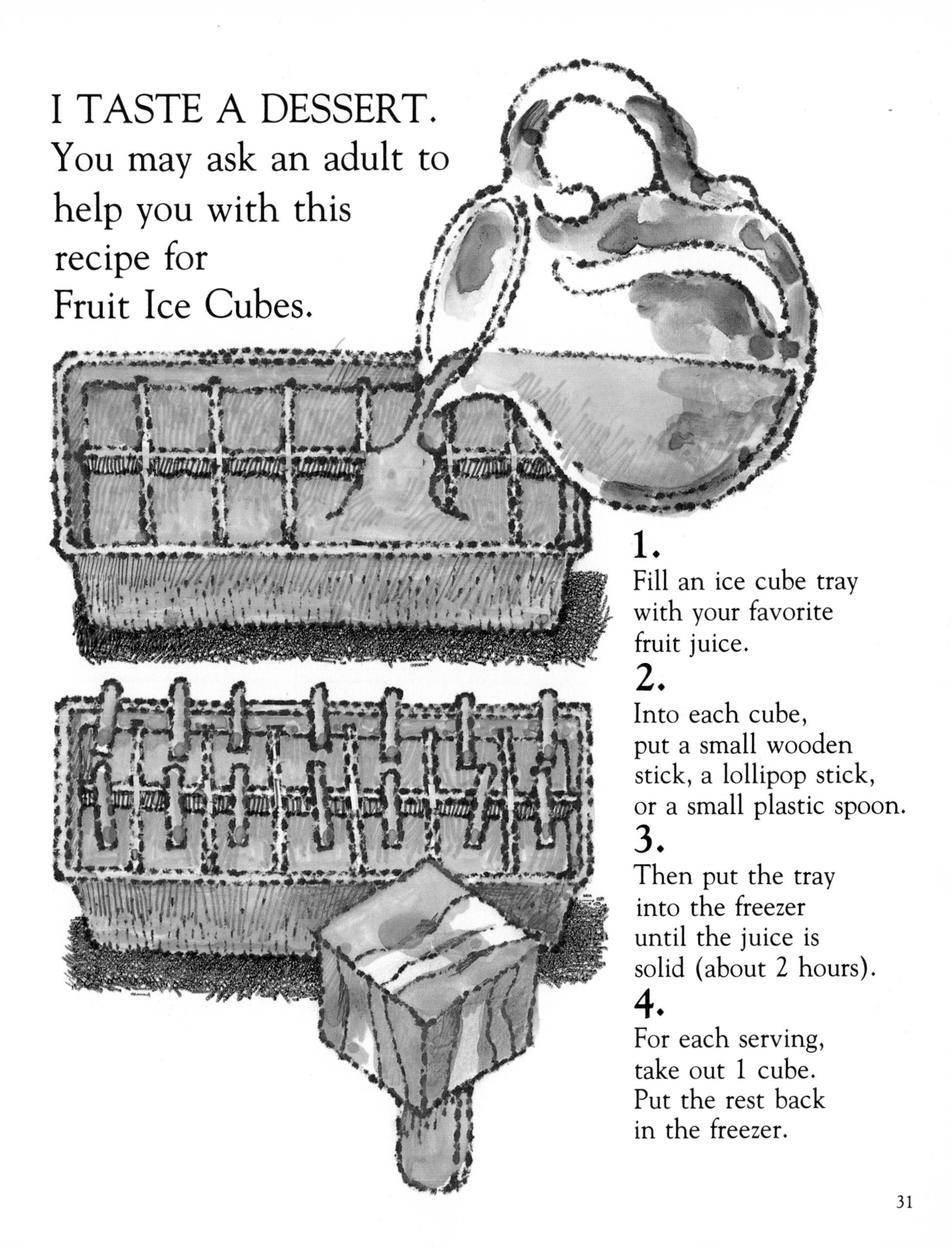

1.
Fill an ice cube tray with your favorite fruit juice.

2.
Into each cube, put a small wooden stick, a lollipop stick, or a small plastic spoon.

3.
Then put the tray into the freezer until the juice is solid (about 2 hours).

4.
For each serving, take out 1 cube. Put the rest back in the freezer.

Ask an adult to help you cut an apple and a potato into small pieces. Shut your eyes and hold your nose closed with your fingers. Have someone put either a piece of apple or a piece of potato into your mouth. Can you tell which one it is?

Try the exact same test — only this time, use pieces of pear and pieces of onion. Now can you tell which is which?

What do these 2 tests tell you about your sense of smell and your sense of taste?

You can make your own book about tasting. Look through a newspaper or magazine. Find pictures of food that you like to taste. Cut out the pictures. Tape or paste them onto pieces of paper. Fasten the papers together in some kind of order (such as sweet, sour, bitter, and salty). You may ask an adult to help you.